The Privilege (

Mrs. Leo Everett

Alpha Editions

This edition published in 2024

ISBN 9789362517852

Design and Setting By
Alpha Editions
www.alphaedis.com
Email - info@alphaedis.com

Contents

INTRODUCTION

A very suggestive and intriguing title is *"The Privilege of Pain."* Those who know a good deal about the subject will doubtless raise the eyebrow of incredulity, while those who have lived in blissful ignorance will be curious if not wholly sympathetic. When I first heard the essay (since developed into this book) read before an audience of very thoughtful and discriminating women, I fancied, although it awakened the liveliest interest in all present, that there was not entire unanimity as to the essayist's point of view. Several invalids and semi-invalids wore an expression of modest pride in the eloquent plea that physical limitations had not succeeded in stemming the tide of mental and spiritual achievement in the long history of the world's progress. Robust ladies, equal to eight hours' work, and if advisable, eight hours' play, out of the twenty-four, looked a trifle aggrieved, as if the gift of perfect health had been underrated, and the laurels that had always surmounted their shining hair and glowing faces might be wrested from them and placed on paler brows. They had no wish to shorten the list of the essayist's heroes, (Heaven forbid!) but they evidently wished to retire to their private libraries and compile a roll of honor from the merely healthy.

However there was no acrimony in the discussion that followed the reading of the paper nor any desire to withhold honor where honor was so gloriously due.

Those who disbelieved in the validity of pain; those who were convinced that mind is not only superior to, but able to win complete triumph over matter; those who felt that laying hold of the Great Source of Healing and Power would enable them not only to deny but to defy pain, these naturally were not completely in accord with the writer.

Myself, I have always thought that the happy waking after dreamless sleep; the exultation in the new day and its appointed task; the sense of vigor and ability to do whatever opportunity offered; the feeling that one could "run and not be weary, could walk and not faint"—that these were the most precious things that the gods could vouchsafe to mankind,—and yet!— What of the latent powers that wake into life when we look into "the bright face of danger"? Our bodies are not commonly the temples that God intended them to be, and yet often an unquenchable fire burns within; an inner flame that incites to effort and achievement, turns the timid slave into the happy warrior. What if the strength born of overcoming should rescue dormant powers equal to those that exist where there is no effort save that engendered by abounding vitality? After all life is an obstacle race to most of us. Who knows whether the horse could make a spectacular jump had he not often been confronted by bar, gate, hurdle and hedge? I wonder how many great things have been carved, painted, written, conceived, invented, where the creative human being has never suffered, but has been sheltered, lapped in ease, the burden lifted from his shoulders? I wonder if the eye that is seldom wet with tears is ever truly capable of the highest vision?

I think that my own unregenerate watchword would be: "All for health and the world well lost!" so I am by no means a special pleader, even yet, for the "privilege of pain"; but Mrs. Everett's enthusiasm and the ardor of her conviction compels a new and more sympathetic understanding of her thesis.

I have more often seen spiritual than intellectual exaltation follow pain, but both were present in one woman, half-poet, half-saint, whose verses were written in intense suffering, as indeed were most of W. E. Henley's.

With closed eyes and pale lips she once quoted to me:

"Angel of Pain! I think thy face

Will be in all the Heavenly Place

The earliest face that I shall see

And swiftest face to smile on me!"

"How is it possible for you to say it?" I asked brokenly.

"Because," she answered, "all dreams and all visions have come to me, as well as all that I know of earth and heaven, through pain. It opens windows in what would otherwise be blank walls!"

The blind, deaf, dumb, maimed, crippled (if so be it the soul is strong) seem to develop a splendid fighting spirit unknown to those who, apparently, have complete command of all their powers. Take one sense away and the others spring, full-armored, into more active service. Rob them of a right hand and the underrated left becomes doubly skilful. These are soldiers in the "army with banners," and should be led and followed by acclaiming hosts.

I have known hundreds of invalids more or less saintly, but I have had personal friendship with only two completely joyous, triumphant ones,—Robert Louis Stevenson and Helen Keller. If "one with God is a majority," then two such conquering human creatures as these furnish inspiration for our generation, and Mrs. Everett in her eager search has found hundreds of similar examples. For that reason I call this a unique, gallant, courageous, helpful little book, likely to give pluck and spirit to many readers handicapped by various ills! There is nothing patient, meek, or resigned in its pages; no air of being crushed-but-still-smiling; it simply radiates a plucky, chin-in-the-air atmosphere calculated to make an aching hand pick up its pen, brush, lump of clay or shovel and go to work; not grimly and doggedly, with lips set, but glowing in triumph over the secret adversary.

The magnificent company marshalled by Mrs. Everett has an exhilarating effect upon the hearer or reader. As I listened to instance after instance of weakness gloriously transmuted into strength; of personal grief and sorrow turned into joy for the whole world; of vast knowledge, spiritual and intellectual, amassed bit by bit in the very grip of physical suffering, I remembered the poetic pronouncement in Revelation.

"He that hath an ear let him hear what the Spirit saith unto the churches; To him that overcometh will I give to eat of the tree of life which is in the midst of the paradise of God."

KATE DOUGLAS WIGGIN

New York, May, 1920.

I
HEALTH AND STRENGTH

Several years ago one of the New York papers published an interview with a well-known physician, on the advisability of women being drafted for war. He expressed himself in favor of their receiving military training, although, he casually remarked, "a good many would undoubtedly perish. But," he argued, "if we blot out the individual equation and judge from the standpoint of race, would their perishing be regrettable?" He thinks not. "For, objectors must remember," he continues, "that mental and moral man gets his strength and efficiency only from the physical man. A sick man, just as a sick race, is the one that goes to the wall."

This outrageous statement was published at the very height of the world war, when men without arms, legs, eyes, men permanently shattered in health, men who will hide all their lives behind masks, were crawling home in hordes. And the worst of it is, that practically everybody agrees with his verdict.

We offer these heroes, who have sacrificed their splendid young bodies on the altar of humanity, a few fine phrases about glory and honor, yet are smugly content to allow them to be crushed by our degrading conviction that the heights of achievement are no longer for them.

Now if a sick race could exist at all, it might go to the wall as the doctor prophesies; but when he narrows his contention to the individual, when he declares that "a sick man goes to the wall," he is venturing a statement which only a surprising ignorance can excuse.

For what is more surprising than for an educated man, a physician, to put forward a claim which can be refuted by anyone who has even a superficial knowledge of the past? Every one I have questioned has been able to recall at least one invalid who has attained celebrity. For instance, all but the unlettered are familiar with the fact that both Keats and Robert Louis Stevenson were diseased.

The vast majority, however, even of cultivated people, do not seem to realize what an extraordinarily large percentage of the greatest men and women have been physically handicapped. It is the joyous mission of this book to prove to all invalids, but more especially to those living victims of the Great War, that Keats and Stevenson, far from representing isolated instances of achievement despite bodily infirmities, are but members of a gallant army, some of whom have reached even greater heights in spite of more painful disabilities.

The relation of insanity to genius has not escaped the notice of scholars, who have already exhaustively dealt with it. I intend therefore to confine myself to those giants of the past who have suffered either from disease, mutilation or constitutional debility. If I have cited a few who have been afflicted with attacks of insanity, I have selected only those whose best work was done after recovering from such seizures, and have carefully excluded all who have had to pay with their intellects the price of a too stupendous vision. I wish furthermore to impress upon you that of all the illustrious men and women I shall enumerate there is not one whose fullest development was not coincident with ill-health, or reached after joining the ranks of the physically unfit.

If we scrutinize more closely this heterogeneous assemblage, we shall discover that it is composed of representatives of the most varied forms of human endeavor,—Saint and philosopher, poet and scientist, author and statesman, musician and artist, and, what is really astonishing, some of the greatest soldiers and one, at least, of the greatest sailors are among them.

II
SOLDIERS AND A SAILOR

Of all vocations, the profession of arms is the one for which it might be supposed that a perfect physique is the most essential.

Yet Alexander, Cæsar, Alfred the Great, John of Bohemia, Torstensson, Le Grand Condé and his great rival Turenne, Luxembourg, Napoleon, General Wolfe and finally Lord Nelson are proofs to die contrary.

Alexander the Great, singular even among men of action for the splendor of his imagination, was an epileptic. So also was Julius Cæsar. The latter was often attacked by his malady on the very field of battle.

Alfred, so justly called "the Great," was stricken in his twentieth year by a mysterious disease which caused him intense pain and from which he was never afterwards free. The extent and diversity of his activities are, however, almost incredible. He excelled as a soldier, politician and administrator. He was also a scholar, and the revival of learning which took place under his reign was due solely to his efforts.

King John of Bohemia stands out as the most romantic and chivalrous figure of the Middle Ages. He dazzled his contemporaries by his exploits and his reputation for valor has never been exceeded. He was overtaken by blindness at the age of forty-three, but, strapped to his horse, continued to lead his armies to battle. For six years this blind hero successfully resisted all the attacks of the Emperor Louis and his allies. His heroic death at the battle of Creçy was a fitting conclusion to a gallant life. According to Camden, the ostrich feathers and the motto "Ich dien," borne ever since by the Prince of Wales, originally formed the crest of King John, and were first assumed by the Black Prince as a token of the admiration with which his antagonist inspired him.

Condé, known to history as "Le Grand Condé," was so delicate in childhood that he was not expected to reach maturity, and his nervous system was "at no time to be trifled with." During his innumerable campaigns he was a constant martyr to fevers and other maladies, but these seldom interfered with his untiring energy or his capacity for work. He had also the power of arousing the enthusiasm of his followers. They said of him: "In the midst of misfortune Condé always maintains the character of a hero."

Turenne is one of the captains whose campaigns Napoleon recommended all soldiers to "read and re-read." Physical infirmities and an impediment in his speech hampered his career in youth. However, by devoting himself to bodily exercises, he succeeded in a measure in overcoming his weaknesses, but to the end he never possessed a normal physique.

Count Torstensson, the brilliant Swedish field-marshal, celebrated after Gustavus Adolphus as the hero of the Thirty Years' War, and compared to Napoleon for the rapidity with which he was able to move his troops, had frequently to lead his army from a litter, as his infirmities would not permit him to mount a horse. He is considered by experts to have been a greater man than his opponent, Tilly, although the latter, strangely enough, has a more widespread reputation.

A propos Luxembourg and William III (although the latter should be included among the statesmen), I will quote a passage from Macaulay. "In such an age (1694) bodily vigor is the most indispensable qualification for a warrior. At the battle of Landon two poor, sickly beings, who, in a rude state of society, would have been considered too puny to bear part in combats, were the souls of two great armies." And further on: "It is probable that the two feeblest in body among the hundred and twenty thousand soldiers that fought at Neerwinden were the hunch-backed dwarf (Luxembourg) who urged forward the fiery onset of France, and the asthmatic skeleton (William III) who covered the slow retreat of England."

Napoleon was an epileptic and Lord Nelson, at the height of his efficiency, had lost an arm and an eye and what is even more remarkable was, so it is said, sick every time he went to sea or whenever the weather was exceptionally rough.

General Wolfe, although only thirty-two years old, was already a man of shattered health when he undertook his famous expedition against Quebec. In spite of disheartening failures and the torture of an internal malady, he finally won the decisive victory which wrested Quebec from the French. During the battle he was twice wounded but refused to leave the field until a third bullet pierced his lung. He survived only long enough to give a final order for cutting off the retreat and breathed his last murmuring: "Now, God be praised, I will die in peace."

Let us consider for a moment what made these men pre-eminent. It was not courage. Cæsar and Napoleon were no braver than thousands of their followers. Nor was it the capacity for endurance. What then was the secret of their power? I answer unhesitatingly,—imagination. No leader has been without it and the greatest leaders are the men who have had it to a superlative degree. Napoleon recognized its mysterious sway, for it was he who said: "Imagination rules the world." Now, imagination is the very quality we find most frequently allied to ill-health.

I beg to call to your attention that with the exception of le grand Condé and possibly Napoleon, not one of these men would have passed his "medical."

It is certainly curious that the profession of arms, the most physically exacting of all professions, is the only one whose greatest examples have without exception been tainted with disease.

III
ILL-HEALTH AND ITS RELATION TO GENIUS

"The physical conditions which accompany and affect what we call genius are obscure, and have hitherto attracted little but empirical notice. It is impossible not to see that absolutely normal man or woman, as we describe normality, is very rarely indeed an inventor, or a seer, or even a person of remarkable mental energy. The bulk of what are called entirely 'healthy' people add nothing to the sum of human achievement, and it is not the average navvy who makes a Darwin nor a typical daughter of the plough who develops into an Elizabeth Barrett Browning.... The more closely we study, with extremely slender resources of evidence, the lives of great men of imagination and action since the beginning of the world, the more clearly we ought to recognize that a reduction of all types to one stolid uniformity of what is called 'health' would have the effect of depriving humanity of precisely those individuals who have added most to the beauty and variety of human existence.... When the physical conditions of men of the highest celebrity in the past are touched upon, it is usual to pass them over with indifference, or else to account for them as the result of disease. The peculiarities of Pascal, or of Pope, or of Michelangelo are either denied, or it is presumed that they were the result of purely morbid factors against which their genius, their rectitude, or their common sense more or less successfully contended. It is admitted that Tasso had a hypersensitive constitution, which cruelty tortured into melancholia, but it is taken for granted that he would have been a greater poet, if he had taken plenty of out-door exercise."

These are the conclusions of Mr. Edmund Gosse, and they are even more radical than mine. It is, however, true that in sickness the perceptions, physical, mental and spiritual, become supernormally acute, and this extreme sensitiveness to impression is one of the attributes of genius. It follows, therefore, that imagination is stimulated by suffering, but not that suffering creates genius or is even inseparably allied to it.

The most universal concomitant of genius is the power of concentration and there is nothing that so fosters that quality as ill-health. By forcing us to limit our activities, our human contacts, it automatically eliminates everything that is not the basic essential of each individual.

We may dream of an absolutely balanced man, one equally supreme in mind, body, and spirit, but I do not believe it possible for such a being to exist. It seems to be a law that we must purchase and develop one faculty at the expense of another. Only by excessive application to one restricted form of activity can we excel in it. Genius is not eccentric, it is concentric. The all-round man is the mediocre man. To perfect even a rose, you must mutilate the bush.

Of all the great men of imagination Leonardo da Vinci and Goethe seem to have been the most superabundantly healthy. This was certainly true of Leonardo in his youth, but I cannot help feeling that when he painted Mona Lisa's smile, Pain, the great teacher, was not unknown to him. However, I may be mistaken, and if so, he is the most complete man in the whole history of art, science or literature, for he enjoyed the advantages of health without forfeiting the hypersensitiveness of suffering.

There is no doubt, however, about Goethe. He kept his splendid physique to the last, and Goethe was unquestionably a very great man. His gigantic intellect is curiously stimulating. No one else of whom I know, with the exception of Leonardo, has had such a multiple outlook on life. That amazing eye of his dissected as well as comprehended all that it rested upon, and it rested upon almost everything tangible. But the very universality of Goethe's genius is one of its limitations. He gives so much, and yet—there it is, he knows no "half-lights." He never leads one to those shadowy regions where the soul is in travail; he knows nothing of that mysterious tract which lies beyond the last outpost of the intellect. His imagination even in its wildest flights is curiously earthbound. I feel that he was too healthy.

IV
AMONG THE POETS
"THEY LEARN IN SUFFERING WHAT THEY TEACH IN SONG"

Horace was a man of feeble health; Milton was blind; Pope deformed. George Herbert, to whom we owe so many of our most beautiful hymns and anthems, was consumptive. John Donne had an enormous influence on English literature, although, according to Mr. Edmund Gosse, his influence was mostly malign. He was praised by Dryden, paraphrased by Pope, and then completely forgotten for a century. His versification is often harsh, but "behind that fantastic garb of language there is an earnest and vigorous mind, and imagination that harbors fire within its cloudy folds and an insight into the mysteries of spiritual life which is often startling. Donne excels in brief flashes of wit and beauty, and in sudden, daring phrases that have the full perfume of poetry in them." Izaak Walton was his admiring friend and first biographer. Donne was constantly ill during the years of his greatest creative activity, yet this is what he once said, speaking of his illnesses: "The advantage you and my other friends have by my frequent fevers is that I am so much the oftener at the gate of heaven; and, by the solitude and close imprisonment they reduce me to, I am so much the oftener at my prayers, in which you and my other dear friends are not forgotten."

It was owing to ill-health that Coleridge first took opium under the guise of a patent medicine.

William Cowper early showed a tendency to melancholia, but it was not until he was almost thirty that the prospects of having to appear at the bar of the House of Lords, preliminary to taking up the position of clerk—a mere formality—drove him completely insane. He attempted suicide and was sent to an asylum where he spent eighteen months. At the age of forty-two he had another attack from which it took him almost three years to recover completely. Nevertheless we find him three years later making his first appearance as an author with "Olney Hymns," written in conjunction with a friend. This was followed by a collection of poems, which was badly received, one critic declaring that "Mr. Cowper was certainly a good, pious man, but without one spark of poetic fire." It was not until 1785 when he was already fifty-four years old and had been twice declared insane that he published the book that was to make him famous. It is entitled: "The Task, Tircinium or a Review of Schools, and the History of John Gilpin." Cowper is among the poets who are epoch-makers. "He brought a new spirit into English verse. With him begins the 'enthusiasm for humanity,' that was afterwards to become so marked in the poetry of Burns, Shelley, Wordsworth and Byron."

Keats suffered from consumption and it is interesting to note that the progress of his disease coincided with the expansion of his genius.

Chatterton is the most astounding and precocious figure in the whole history of letters. He was only seventeen years and nine months old when starvation drove him to commit suicide, "but the best of his numerous productions, both in prose and verse, require no allowance to be made for the immaturity of their author." Chatterton's audience has never been a large one for the reason that with a few exceptions all his poems are written in Fifteenth Century English. Among the discriminating, however, he holds a very high place. His genius and tragic death are commemorated by Wordsworth in "Resolution and Independence," by Coleridge in "A Monody on the Death of Chatterton," by D. G. Rossetti in "Five English Poets," and Keats dedicated "Endymion" to his memory.

I have hesitated as to whether I had a right to include Chatterton among my examples, because I can find no record of his having suffered from actual disease. On the other hand he was so abnormal that I feel that I have no right to ignore him. From his earliest years he was subject to fits of abstraction during which he would sit for hours in seeming stupor from which it was almost impossible to wake him. For a time he was even considered deficient in intellect.

Thomas Hood was a chronic invalid; his most famous poem, "The Bridge of Sighs," was written on his death-bed. Byron and Swinburne were also physically handicapped.

W. E. Henley was not only a poet but a trenchant critic and a successful editor. A physical infirmity forced him at the age of twenty-five to become an inmate of an Edinburgh hospital. While there he wrote a number of poems in irregular rhythm describing, with poignant force, his experiences as a patient. Sent to the *Cornhill Magazine*, they at once aroused the interest of Leslie Stephen, the editor, and induced him to visit the young poet and to take Robert Louis Stevenson with him. This meeting in the hospital and the friendship which ensued between Stevenson and Henley were famous in the literary gossip of the last century. Henley's reputation will rest on his poetry, and the best of his poems will retain a permanent place in English literature. As a literary editor he displayed a gift for discovering men of promise, and "Views and Reviews" is a "volume of notable criticism."

Sidney Lanier, one of the most original and talented of American poets, was consumptive, and Francis Thompson, author of "The Hound of Heaven," wrote his flaming verse under acute pain.

The Sixteenth Century was the heyday of poets. Princes regarded them as the chief ornament of their courts and disputed among themselves the honor of their company. Ronsard's life, therefore, was exceptionally fortunate. He enjoyed the favor of the three sons of Catherine de' Medici, more especially of Charles IX, after whose premature death the poet retired from Paris. Ronsard is celebrated as the chief glory of an association of poets who called themselves the "Pléiade." His own generation bestowed upon him the title of "Prince of Poets." Ronsard became deaf at eighteen and so he became a man of letters instead of a diplomatist. His infirmity is probably responsible for a "certain premature agedness, a tranquil, temperate sweetness" which characterizes the school of poetry he founded.

Joachim du Bellay was destined for the army and his poetry would most probably have been lost to the world if he had not been attacked by a serious illness which seemed likely to prove fatal. It was during the idle days of his convalescence that he first read the Greek and Latin poets. He was also a member of the "Pléiade" and some of his isolated pieces excel those of Ronsard in "airy lightness of touch."

Molière is the greatest name in French literature. The facts as to his youth and early manhood are so wrapped in uncertainty, that it is impossible to say when the frailty of his health first became manifest. When he emerges from obscurity we find him already subject to attacks of illness and forced to limit himself to a milk diet. His best work, however, was still undone. "Tartuffe" was not written until 1664 when Molière was already forty-two years old, and "Le Misanthrope" was performed a year later. Although it had probably long been latent, he first showed unmistakable symptoms of consumption in 1667. In spite of the ravages of disease, and the continual strain of an impossible domestic situation, he produced "Le Bourgois Gentilhomme" three years later, followed by "Les Fourberies de Scapin." "Le Malade Imaginaire" was written shortly before his death, and it was while acting the title rôle that he ruptured a blood vessel. He died a few hours afterwards, alone, except for the casual presence of two Sisters of Charity.

Scarron, poet, dramatist and novelist, lived twenty years in a state of miserable deformity and pain. His head and body were twisted; his legs useless. He bore his sufferings with invincible courage. Scarron was a prominent figure in the literary and fashionable society of his day. His work, however, is very unequal. That the "Roman Burlesque" is a novel of real merit, no competent critic can deny. It was republished during the nineteenth century, not only in the original French but in an English translation. Scarron is also of interest as the first husband of the lady who as Mme. de Maintenon became the wife of Louis XIV.

Boileau was the youngest of fifteen children. He is said to have had but one passion, the hatred of stupid books. He was the first critic to demonstrate the poetical possibilities of the French language. His two masterpieces are "L'Art Poétique" and "Lutrin." "After much depreciation Boileau's critical work has been rehabilitated and his judgments have been substantially adopted by his successors." He suffered all his life from constitutional debility.

Schiller was a leading spirit of his age, yet from his thirty-second year "every one of his nerves was an avenue of pain." Nevinson, however, considered "it possible the disease served in some way to increase Schiller's eager activity and fan his intellect into keener flame." Carlyle also writes of the poet that "in the midst of his infirmities he persevered with unabated zeal in the great business of his life. His frame might be impaired, but his spirit retained its fire unextinguished." Schiller wrote some of his noblest and greatest plays during the periods of his most acute suffering. When he died it was found that all his vital organs were deranged.

Heinrich Heine, another immortal, spent eight years of his agitated struggling life on what he called "a mattress-grave." "These years of suffering seem to have effected what might be called a spiritual purification of Heine's nature, and to have brought out all the good side of his character, whereas adversity in earlier days had only emphasized his cynicism." Though crippled and racked with constant pain, his intellectual and creative powers were no whit dimmed. His greatest poems were written during these years of suffering from which he found relief only in death.

Petrarch suffered from epilepsy, and Alfieri, one of the greatest of the Italian tragic poets, was a martyr to pain. So likewise was Leopardi, author of some immortal odes; the latter was, furthermore, deformed. It was said of him that "Pain and Love are the two-fold poetry of his existence."

Camoens, the greatest of Portuguese poets, lost his right eye attempting to board an enemy ship. After a life of incredible hardship, he died in a public almshouse worn out by disease.

There are hardly any women poets, which is rather curious, as it is almost the only career that requires neither training nor paraphernalia, yet among this handful we find four, three of them being of real importance, namely: Mrs. Browning, Christina Rossetti and Emily Dickinson. Mrs. Browning was a chronic invalid and wrote her greatest poems, "Sonnets from the Portuguese," while actually on her back. Mr. Edmund Gosse says of

Christina Rossetti, "All we really know about her, save that she was a great saint, was that she was a great poet." She was also a great sufferer.

The most curious event of American literary history was the sudden rise of Emily Dickinson into a posthumous fame. This strange woman, who shunned publicity with a morbid terror and never left her "father's house for any house or town," nevertheless bequeathed to the world poems which for life and fire are unexcelled. She was an invalid. In 1863 she writes: "I was ill since September, and since April in Boston for a physician's care. He does not let me go, yet I work in my prison, and make guests for myself. Carlo (her dog) did not come, because he would die in jail and the mountains I could not hold now, so I brought but the gods!"

Frances Ridley Havergal wrote some of her most beautiful hymns on a sick bed.

V
NOVELISTS

The first name I find on my list of novelists who have been subject to ill health is that of Cervantes. He did not start life an invalid,—far from it. He seems to have been a youth of unusual vigor. But when only twenty-three years old he was severely wounded and lost his left hand in battle—"For the greater glory of the right," as he gallantly exclaimed. After that he spent five years in slavery and he escaped from the Moors only to languish at various times in a Spanish prison. Hardship, and privations doubtless, and also his old wounds, had completely shattered his health when he finally sat down to create his immortal "Don Quixote." The first part was published when he was fifty-eight years old, the last when he was sixty-nine.

When Fielding wrote "Tom Jones," he had been for years a martyr to gout and other diseases: Gibbon predicted for this work "a diuturnity exceeding that of the house of Austria!" It is curious that this book, which bubbles over with the joy of life, was written at a time when Fielding was plunged into the deepest melancholy.

Swift suffered from "labyrinthian vertigo."

Laurence Sterne, creator of "Tristram Shandy," was consumptive, as he says of himself, "from the first hour I drew breath unto this that I can hardly breathe at all." Sterne, no longer young, was increasingly suffering during the years he brought forth the numerous volumes of his unique book.

Sir Walter Scott was not only lame from infancy but is an inspiring example of what can be accomplished under conditions of extreme physical suffering. When he was forty-six years old began a series of agonizing attacks of cramps of the stomach which recurred at frequent intervals for two years. But his activity and capacity for work remained unbroken. He made his initial attempt at play-writing when he was recovering from this first seizure. Before the year was out he had completed "Rob Roy." Within six months it was followed by "The Heart of Midlothian," which filled four volumes of the second series of "Tales of my Landlord," and has remained one of the most popular among his novels. "The Bride of Lammermoor" and "The Legend of Montrose" were dictated to amanuenses, through fits of suffering so acute that he could not suppress cries of agony. When Laidlaw begged him to stop dictating he only answered, "Nay, Willie, only see that the doors are fast. I would fain keep all the cry, as well as all the wool to ourselves, but to give over work, that can only be when I am woolen."

Mme. de La Fayette lost her health a year before her epoch-making novel, "La Princess de Cléves," was published. She lived fifteen years afterwards, "étant de ceux," as Sainte-Beuve says, "qui traînent leur miserable vie jusqu'à la dernière goutte d'huile." "La Princesse de Cléves" is not only intrinsically a work of real merit, which is still read with pleasure, but is important because it is the first novel of sentiment, the first novel, in the sense we moderns use the word, that was ever written.

Le Sage was a handsome, engaging youth, but it was not until he was thirty-nine years old that he made his first success with the "Diable Boiteux." Already his deafness was rapidly increasing; and he was sixty-seven years old and had long been completely deaf when the last volume of the masterpiece, "Gil Blas," appeared.

Vauvenargues was a soldier until he had both of his legs frozen during a winter campaign. This injury, from which he never recovered, forced him to leave the army. An attack of small-pox completed the ruin of his health, and thenceforth he led a secluded life devoted to literary pursuits. It is mainly as a novelist that Vauvenargues occupies a place in French literature, although his other works were held in high esteem by his contemporaries.

Edmond and Jules de Goncourt are names famous in French literary history. "Learning something from Flaubert, and teaching almost everything to Zola, they invented a new kind of novel, and their works are the result of a new vision of the world…. A novel of the Goncourts is made up of an infinite number of details, set side by side, every detail equally prominent…. French critics have complained that the language of the Goncourts is no longer the French of the past, and this is true. It is their distinction, the finest of their inventions, that in order to render new sensations, a new vision of things, they invented a new language." (Mr. Arthur Symons.) Their journal is a gold mine from which present-day writers still carry away unacknowledged nuggets. M. Paul Bourget said of them: "Life reduced itself to a series of epileptic attacks, preceded and followed by a blank."

Dostoievsky is considered by many critics the greatest of the great Russian novelists.

His health was completely shattered by his spending four years in a Siberian prison as a political offender. This terrible experience, however, served to create "Recollections of a Dead House" and "Buried Alive in Siberia."

Anton Chekhov, the Russian novelist and short story writer, was only a little over twenty when he began to suffer from attacks of blood spitting.

Although he believed that these came from his throat they were undoubtedly due to consumption. He was also a martyr to digestive trouble and headaches.

Chekhov possessed to an unusual degree the nervous energy which so frequently accompanies disease. He was a remarkably prolific author, so much so that in one of his letters he prophesies that he will soon have written enough to fill a library with his own works. Literature was, however, not his only pursuit. He also practiced medicine, although he refused to receive any remuneration for his services. He was public spirited and altruistic and organized an association for the relief of Siberian prisoners.

His books enjoy an immense vogue and have been translated into every language.

Whatever may be the future of English fiction, Charlotte Brontë's novels will always command attention, by reason of their intensity and individuality. She suffered from permanent bodily weakness with various complications.

Some critics consider Emily Brontë superior to her sister. "Wuthering Heights" is a "thing apart, passionate, unforgettable." This remarkable book was written while its author was dying of consumption.

That super-woman, known to fame as George Eliot, suffered all her life from frequent attacks of illness. In spite of her physical limitations she was capable of the most prolonged and intense application. Her numerous novels, dating from her thirty-sixth year, are only a part of her widespread intellectual activities.

Jacobsen, the great Danish novelist, unfortunately too little known in this country, was, like so many others, cut off from his chosen or destined profession and driven into literature by ill health. During the worst phases of his sufferings he produced books that in their way have never been surpassed.

I must mention here, though she belongs to no category, that extraordinary child, Marie Bashkirtseff, who, dying of consumption at twenty-four, left behind her several pictures of great promise (two of them are in the Luxembourg Gallery, I believe) and her "Journal," a remarkable production which created a sensation thirty years ago and which has lately been republished.

Robert Louis Stevenson's life is so well-known that I need only to recall him to your memory.

Henry James was so delicate that he was forced to remain a spectator of the Civil War, in which his younger brothers fought. Mr. Edmund Gosse writes the following description of a visit to Henry James when the latter was already thirty-two years old. "Stretched on a sofa and apologizing for not rising to greet me, his appearance gave me a little shock, for I had not thought of him as an invalid. He hurriedly and rather evasively declared that he was not that, but that a muscular weakness of the spine obliged him, as he said, 'to assume a horizontal posture during some hours of every day in order to bear an almost unbroken routine of evening engagements.'" It is recorded that in one winter he dined out one hundred and seven times. What amazing assiduity! His health gradually grew stronger, but for many years it seriously handicapped his activity.

I should like to linger a moment with Lafcadio Hearn. He is known to the world at large as the foremost interpreter of the old and new Japan. He married a Japanese wife and this gave him a peculiar insight into the customs as well as the psychology of his adopted countrymen. His books show a unique understanding of the Oriental mind and their literary art is exquisite. He not only suffered from ill health, but in addition lost the sight of one eye in early youth and ever after went in fear of total blindness. Yet, far from regretting his afflictions, this is what he said about them: "The owner of pure horse-health never purchased the power of discerning the half-lights. In its separation of the spiritual from the physical portion of existence, severe sickness is often invaluable to the sufferer, in the revelation it bestows of the psychological undercurrents of human existence. From the intuitive recognition of the terrible but at the same time glorious fact, that the highest life can only be reached by subordinating physical to spiritual influences, separating the immaterial from the material self,—therein lies all the history of asceticism and self-suppression as the most efficacious measure of developing religious and intellectual power." That is what experience had taught one who was certainly not a religionist.

VI
PHYSICAL PERFECTION AND ITS RELATION TO CIVILIZATION

I am persuaded that it is impossible to banish suffering from the world. All we have so far accomplished is to exchange one form of suffering for another.

Take the case of women, for example, and the ailments to which they are subject. Primitive woman was virtually free from these. She suffered little at childbirth. To-day the operation of even the normal female functions has become a serious matter. Science with all its strides has not been able to cope successfully with the increasing burden which the conditions of modern life impose on woman's physique.

I have chosen women as an illustration because they themselves would be the first to insist that they had profited more than men from the advance of thought and the perfecting of a social system that is largely their own creation. Well, compare this Flower of the Ages, as we see her in shops, offices, ball-rooms or even colleges, with an Australian bush-woman, and we will find that neither in health, strength nor endurance can she rival her savage sister. The woman of the bush is capable of following her master all day with a baby on her back; of stopping for a brief period to produce another and of resuming her progress, unimpeded by her additional burden.

It is well to realize that civilization, which has bestowed such incalculable benefits upon mankind, has done so largely at the expense of its physical welfare. Moreover, as men, and more particularly women, rise in the intellectual scale, they risk the sacrifice not only of a robust, but of a normal, body. But what of it? "Wisdom is better than strength; and a wise man is better than a strong man." Nor must we forget that while civilization has undoubtedly undermined our physique, it has also abolished the circumstances which made strength and endurance the supreme necessities of the battle of life. To be able to follow her male with a child on her back—to say nothing of the interesting interlude—is not a quality that would add either to the allurement or efficiency of the woman of to-day.

Let me here cite four celebrated women who, differing from each other in every other particular, suffered in common from ill health.

The first in order of time is Madame du Deffand who was for many years the center of one of the most brilliant of the Eighteenth Century salons.

Her correspondence with Voltaire, La Duchesse Choiseul and Horace Walpole is immortal and has been frequently republished. Many of her letters to Voltaire and all of those to Mme. de Choiseul and Horace Walpole were dictated when she was over sixty-seven years of age, broken in health and totally blind.

Rachel was the daughter of a poor Jew pedlar, and from the age of four she roamed the streets singing patriotic songs. A famous singing teacher heard her and, impressed by the crude power of the little creature, offered to teach her gratuitously. It is almost unbelievable to read of the excitement this small, plain Jewess created. She still lives in hundreds of books and is an integral part of the history of her period. If we can judge from contemporary praises, Rachel is the greatest actress of whom there is any record. She suffered from continual ill health and died of consumption in her thirty-seventh year.

Grace Darling was the daughter of a lighthouse keeper, and with her father braved almost certain death in attempting to save the survivors of the wreck of the *Forfarshire*. By well-nigh superhuman efforts they succeeded in rescuing a great number. This gallant exploit made them both famous. Grace Darling had always been delicate and died of consumption four years later.

Florence Nightingale, immortal nurse and one of the most influential women in history, had at the time of her greatest activity a body so weak that it was a wonder how a woman in such delicate health was able to perform so much of what Sidney Herbert called "a man's work." During many years of important achievement she was altogether bed-ridden. Working incessantly, writing, organizing, she was a power throughout the British Empire. Her influence has spread over the world; to her we owe the first idea of training nurses.

It is really curious that physical fitness should have become an ideal only after it had ceased to be the indispensable requirement of our environment. Piano-moving is perhaps the sole occupation to-day where strength is the only qualification, and intelligence of no account whatsoever; yet few of us aspire to become piano-movers!

The body is a most delicate machine and only in exceptional cases can it be kept through life in perfect condition, without an immense expenditure of time and trouble. Now, a perfect body should only be considered desirable, if it enables us to rise to greater heights of achievement. Countless people, however, regard health and vigor not merely as the means but as the goal itself. They tend and exercise their bodies at the expense of every other form of activity. The disproportionate amount of time, energy and aspiration that is wasted in attempting to perfect and preserve that which is inevitably doomed to destruction is incredible. A child building a castle on the sand is engaged in a more durable occupation. For the child, while erecting its tunnelled and turreted fortress, is at least attempting to realize some haunting dream of the heights, the depths, the mystery and magnificence of life. What matter the tide?—the vision is indestructible.

The Greeks regarded a beautiful body as an end in itself, because their civilization, by permitting its unveiling, allowed it to act as an inspiration to others. The nude, however, has no recognized place among us, and although it still serves to create beauty, it does so under restricted and abnormal conditions. To be a model is not a title to fame, nor the ideal of our most enlightened contemporaries.

I hope that I have proved conclusively that a splendid body is no longer a necessary means of enabling us to rise to the greatest heights either of ambition or of service. Why, therefore, should we so morbidly covet physical perfection?

VII
THE PHYSICALLY HANDICAPPED PHILOSOPHERS

Τὸν φρονεῖν βροτοὺς ὁδώσαντα τὸν πάθει μάθος θέντα κυρίως ἔχειν.

—*Aeschylus, Agememnon, line 186.*

Among the British philosophers who were physical sufferers we find the great Francis Bacon, who from childhood was always weak and delicate.

John Locke became world-famous by reason of his still celebrated "Essay concerning Human Understanding." He was also of political importance, having occupied for years the position of confidential adviser to the great Earl of Shaftesbury. Professor Campbell says of him: "Locke is apt to be forgotten now, because in his own generation he so well discharged the intellectual mission of initiating criticism of human knowledge, and of diffusing the spirit of free enquiry and universal toleration which has since profoundly affected the civilized world. He has not bequeathed an imposing system, hardly even a striking discovery in metaphysics, but he is a signal example in the Anglo-Saxon world of the love of attainable truth for the sake of truth and goodness. If Locke made few discoveries, Socrates made none. But both are memorable in the record of human progress."

Robert Boyle, the natural philosopher, was the seventh son and fourteenth child of the great Earl of Cork. His scientific work procured him extraordinary reputation among his contemporaries. It was he who "first enunciated the law that the volume of gas varies inversely as the pressure, which among English-speaking people is still called by his name." Great as were his attainments they were almost over-shadowed by the saintliness of his character, the liveliness of his wit and the incomparable charm of his manner. Boyle was a man of the most feeble health. This is what Evelyn says of him: "The contexture of his body seemed to me so delicate that I have frequently compared him to Venice glass, ... [which] though wrought never so fine, being carefully set up, would outlast harder metals of daily use."

Robert Hooke, the experimental philosopher, was both deformed and diseased. He was not a great man and his scientific achievements would have been "more striking if they had been less varied." Nevertheless he was renowned in his day, and his contribution of real importance for, although "he perfected little he originated much." I mention him, and shall mention several others, who have been forgotten by all but scholars, because I wish to show how large an army stands behind its illustrious chiefs. Besides, if we contemplate only the giant luminaries of the firmament of fame, we shall become discouraged. They paralyze us by the very intensity of the admiration they evoke. Lesser men, on the contrary, for the reason that they are nearer our own orbit, are more likely to stir us into emulation.

Herbert Spencer's achievements are too well known to necessitate further comment. He was exceedingly delicate and at his best only able to work three hours a day.

Descartes, the foremost French philosopher, had a feeble and somewhat abnormal body. "Yet he considered it" (I am quoting Mr. Edmund Gosse) "well suited to his own purposes, and was convinced that the Cartesian philosophy would not have been improved, though the philosopher's digestion might, by developing the thews of a plough-boy."

Nicholas Malebranche, the great French Cartesian philosopher, was the tenth child of his parents. Although deformed and constitutionally feeble he was one of the most sought after men of his day. From all countries of the world, but more especially from England (be it said in her honour) scholars, writers and philosophers flocked to his door. The German princes voyaged to Paris expressly to see him. The philosopher Berkeley was probably the cause of his death by forcing himself on Malebranche when the latter had been ordered absolute quiet. His influence has been variously estimated. Spinoza is undoubtedly one of his disciples. Mons. Emile Faguet says of him: "Malebranche est un des plus beaux (metaphysiciens) que j'aie rencontrés. Si l'on veut ma pensée, je trouve Descartes plus grand savant et plus vaste ésprit; mais je trouve Malebranche plus grand philosophe, d'un degré au moins que Descartes lui-Même." Speaking of his character he writes: "Il n'y eut jamais homme de plus d'ésprit, ni plus homme de bien, ni plus seduisant."

Blaise Pascal, the great French religious philosopher, still holds a position of immense importance in the history of literature as well as philosophy. His "Provincial Letters" are the "first example of polite controversial irony since Lucian and they have continued to be the best example of it during more than two centuries in which style has been sedulously practised and in which they have furnished a model to generation after generation." His "Pensées," published after his death, is "still a favorite exploring ground ... to persons who take an interest in their problems." In philosophy his position is this: "He seized firmly and fully the central idea of the difference between reason and religion, but unlike most men since his day who, not contented with a mere concordat, have let religion go and contented themselves with reason," Pascal, though equally dissatisfied, "held fast to religion and continued to fight out the questions of difference with reason."

From the age of eighteen, Pascal never passed a single day without pain. Nevertheless, in the worst of his sufferings he was wont to say: "Do not pity me; sickness is the natural condition of Christians. In sickness we are as we ought always to be ... in the suffering of pains, in the privation of goods and of all the pleasures of the senses, exempt from all passions which work in us during the whole course of our life, without ambition, without avarice, in the continual expectation of death."

Voltaire suffered frequent attacks of illness. It was said of him that "he was born dying."

Comte, the French Positive philosopher, accomplished the bulk of his work after recovering from an attack of insanity during which he threw himself into the Seine. Perhaps it is too soon to judge of the ultimate value of his system of philosophy. It has had impassioned adherents as well as scornful critics. His main thesis seems to be "that the improvement of social conditions can only be effected by moral development and never by any political mechanism, or any violence in the way of an artificial redistribution of wealth." In other words, he preached that a moral transformation must precede any real advance. Yet he was not a Christian. An enemy defined Comtism as "Catholicism without Christianity."

Henri Frederic Amiel, Swiss philosopher and critic, whose chief work, the "Journal Intime," published after his death, obtained for him European reputation, was a valetudinarian. Amiel wrote but little, but all he accomplished has the quality of exquisite sensitiveness.

The great Kant was a wretched little creature barely five feet high with a concave chest and a deformed right shoulder; his constitution was of the frailest, though by taking extraordinary precautions he escaped serious illness.

VIII
ASTRONOMERS AND MATHEMATICIANS

Johann Kepler, the great German astronomer, was a contemporary of Tycho Brahe and Galileo with both of whom he was in correspondence. Kepler's contributions to science were of the utmost importance. It was he who established the two cardinal principles of modern astronomy—the laws of elliptical orbits and of equal areas. He also enunciated important truths relating to gravity. In spite of the backward condition of mechanical knowledge, he attempted to explain the planetary evolutions by a theory of vortices closely resembling that afterwards adopted by Descartes. He also prepared the way for the discovery of the infinitesimal calculus. His literary remains were purchased by Catherine the Second of Russia and were only published during the latter half of the Nineteenth Century. It is impossible to consider without astonishment the colossal amount of work accomplished by Kepler, despite his great physical disabilities. When only four years old an attack of small-pox had left him with crippled hands and eyesight permanently impaired. His constitution, already enfeebled by premature birth, had to withstand successive shocks of illness.

Flamstead, the great British astronomer, was obliged to leave school in consequence of a rheumatic affection of the joints. It was to solace his enforced idleness that he took up the study of astronomy. The extent and quality of his performance is almost unbelievable when one considers his severe physical suffering.

Nicholas Saunderson lost his sight before he was twelve months old, yet he became professor of mathematics at Cambridge. He was an eminent authority in his day, an original and efficient teacher and the author of a book on algebra. His knowledge of optics was remarkable. "He had distinct ideas of perspective, of the projection of the sphere, and of the forms assumed by plane or solid figures."

D'Alembert was not only a mathematician but also a philosopher of the highest order. He was made a member of the French Academy at the age of twenty-four. He was so frail that his life was continually despaired of and he remained a valetudinarian to the end.

IX
STATESMEN AND POLITICIANS

We now come to the statesmen and politicians. Robert Cecil, first Earl of Salisbury, Secretary of State under Queen Elizabeth and Lord Treasurer under James I, was a statesman who all his life wielded immense power to the undoubted benefit of his country. Yet in person he was in strange contrast to his rivals at court, being deformed and sickly. Elizabeth styled him her pigmy; his enemies vilified him as "wry-neck," "crooked-back" and "splay-foot." In Bacon's essay "Of Deformity" he paints his cousin to the life.

John Somers, Lord Keeper under William and Mary, "was in some respects" (I am quoting Macaulay) "the greatest man of his age. He was equally eminent as a jurist, as a politician and as a writer.... His humanity was the more remarkable because he received from nature a body such as is generally found united to a peevish and irritable mind. His life was one long malady; his nerves were weak; his complexion livid; his face prematurely wrinkled."

William III, I have already mentioned, and now comes a name to conjure with, the great Lord Clive, founder of the British Empire. At eighteen he went out to India and shortly afterwards the effect of the climate on his health began to show itself in those fits of depression during one of which he ended his life. We see in his end the result of physical suffering, of chronic disease which opium failed to abate.

William Pitt, Earl of Chatham, one of the greatest statesmen England ever had, suffered from hereditary gout. The attacks continued from boyhood with increasing intensity to the close of his life. He was for two years mentally unbalanced, yet after that he returned to Parliament and directed for eight years all the power of his eloquence in favor of the American Colonies. Dr. Johnson said: "Walpole was a minister given by the King to the people, but Pitt was a minister given by the people to the King."

Whatever we may think of Marat as a man, we cannot deny that he occupies a large place in the history of his time. Yet he was always delicate, so much so that after the completion of one of his books he lay in a stupor during thirteen days. In 1788 he was attacked by a terrible malady, from which he suffered during the whole of his revolutionary career.

Pitt, the younger, was a sickly child and although he grew into a healthy youth, his constitution was early broken by gout.

Owing to an accident in early childhood Talleyrand was lamed for life. At the time this seemed a great misfortune, for owing to his disability he forfeited his right of primogeniture and the profession of arms was closed to him. "No Frenchman of his age did so much to repair the ravages wrought by fanatics and autocrats."

Henry Fawcett, the English politician and economist, was accidentally blinded at the age of twenty-five. The effect of his blindness was, as the event proved, the reverse of calamitous. By concentrating his energies, it brought his powers to earlier maturity than would otherwise have been possible, and "it had a mellowing influence on his character, which in youth had been rough and canny, and inclined to harshness." Gladstone appointed him Postmaster-General in 1880 and not England alone, but the world as well, is deeply indebted to him for the reforms he inaugurated. He instituted the parcel post, postal orders, sixpenny telegrams, the banking of small savings by means of stamps and increased facilities for life insurance and annuities.

Kavanaugh was an Irish politician and member of the privy council of Ireland. He had only the rudiments of legs and arms but in spite of these physical defects he had a remarkable career. He learned to ride in the most fearless fashion, strapped to a special saddle and managing his horse with the stumps of his arms; he also fished, shot, drew and wrote, various mechanical devices supplementing his limited physical capacities.

X
THE FREEDOM OF ILL-HEALTH

One of the greatest advantages of invalidism is that it frees us from petty obligations, unworthy pleasures, and meaningless conventions. The blessed freedom of ill-health is something few people appreciate; neither have they learned to make full use of its unearned leisure. Yet we are always clamoring for time; in America, apparently, it can be found only in the sickroom.

How many people do we not know, who are so busy making, what they are pleased to call a living, that they never find time to live! As a matter of fact, only the small minority of the inefficient are obliged to sacrifice all possibility of leisure to the exigency of obtaining a livelihood; the majority, which include men and women of every class and of every vocation— plumbers and captains of industry, stenographers as well as débutantes— are occupied in accumulating superfluities. By superfluities I do not mean everything which is not normally necessary for the existence of the body, but everything that is not essential to the perfect expansion of separate individuality.

The tendency of the day is to pour all mankind into the same mould; to fetter great and small to the one ideal of obvious achievement. We have degraded success by popularizing it; we are suppressing individuality instead of fostering it; and unless a change comes before long, and the individual is again able to liberate himself and to germinate, we shall perish as other civilizations have perished without leaving more than a scratch on the page of history. For nations are ultimately judged, not by their numbers, their riches or their power, but solely by the glory of the individuals they have produced. Think of the empires which have so completely vanished that but for a few broken stones we could not even guess the sites of their vast cities, and compare these nations either to the Jews or Greeks who during their flowering gave birth to men who have conferred immortality on their respective races.

Suffering quickens individuality by removing the pressure of circumstance, custom and occupation. Moreover, in the sick-room the intellect as well as the soul has not only the liberty but the time to mature.

It always surprises me to hear people complain of insomnia. Why should they consider it a misfortune to live precious hours instead of spending them in unconsciousness? By sleeping even as much as five hours instead of nine, we gain twenty-one hours a week. Think of it! Almost three working days!

The reason the average person is so exhausted by lying awake a few hours longer that he is accustomed to do, is because he turns and twists in his bed bemoaning his sad fate, until he has worked himself into a fever. Stay awake; enjoy the night,—it is quite as wonderful as the day. Taste the charm of the silence as it steals by degrees over your weary spirit. Be grateful for these hours; they are a gift from fate. Read, write, think, meditate, and when morning comes you will wake more refreshed after two hours' sleep than you used to after nine. Napoleon and other great men never slept more.

XI
ARTISTS

The great painters and sculptors seem to have been strangely healthy and normal. I say that they seem to have been so, because of the extreme difficulty of getting any accurate information on the subject. It sounds incredible, but I read a long life of Petrarch in which everything was mentioned but his health and only discovered quite accidentally that he had been an epileptic.

I am, therefore, convinced that there are many examples I might cite if I could only unearth the truth, yet even so, I have been able to ferret out four artists who were physically handicapped. Navarette, called the Spanish Titian and celebrated under the name of "El Mudo," was dumb. They say that Guercino squinted so badly that he could focus only one eye.

Antoine Watteau suffered all his life from tuberculosis, which no doubt accounts for a certain "wistful gaiety" which characterizes his work. Watteau's position in French art is of unique importance. He became the founder—as the culmination—of a new school which marked a revolt against the pompous classicism of the preceding period. "The vitality of his art was due to the rare combination of a poet's imagination with a power of seizing reality. In his treatment of landscape background and the atmospheric conditions surrounding his figures we find the germ of Impressionism." From the middle of the Eighteenth Century until about 1875 Watteau's work fell into disrepute. It was chiefly owing to the efforts of the brothers de Goncourt that a reaction set in which has slowly carried Watteau to the summit of fame. He died in his thirty-seventh year.

Aubrey Beardsley flashed into fame with black and white drawings of extraordinary originality and beauty. His peculiar technique has been widely imitated but never approached. After twenty years his reputation has not yet reached its zenith. Aubrey Beardsley during the whole of his meteoric career suffered from consumption. He died at the age of twenty-six.

XII
MUSICIANS

One would expect deafness to be an insuperable obstacle to a musician, yet Beethoven produced a large part of his work while handicapped by it, and some of his greatest compositions when his deafness had become complete. Mozart was delicate and subject to fevers; his last work and his best was written just before his death. It was said of Händel: "He was never greater than when, warned by palsy of the approach of death, and struggling with distress and suffering, he sat down to compose the great works which have made his name immortal in music." Schubert was barely five feet one and walked with a strange shuffling gait; his eyesight was so defective that he slept in his spectacles. He suffered from digestive trouble and died young. So also did Chopin, having been an invalid the greater part of his short life. Mendelssohn was very frail and delicate. Carl Maria von Weber was not only ravaged by disease but also deformed and lame. Paganini, the most extraordinary violinist the world has ever heard, suffered from phthisis of the larynx and was constantly ill.

The case of Robert Schumann is very curious. He was studying to be a pianist, when, in attempting to strengthen his fingers, he accidentally paralyzed his right hand. To this apparent misfortune we owe one of the greatest composers.

XIII
THREE PHYSICIANS, A NATURALIST AND A CHEMIST

"Physician, heal thyself," might have been said to Sir William Harvey, the famous discoverer of the circulation of the blood; and to Albert von Haller, the great Swiss doctor, who is considered the father of modern physiology.

To Louis Pasteur the world is indebted for the introductions of methods which have already worked wonders and bid fair to render possible the preventive treatment of all infectious disease. His most sensational discovery was the cure of hydrophobia, which he accomplished despite the fact that the special microbe causing this dread disease had not yet been isolated. Pasteur's motto was, "Travaillez, travaillez toujours." On his death-bed he turned to his devoted pupils and exclaimed: "Où en êtes-vous? Que faîtes-vous?" and ended by repeating: "Il faut travailler." He once said: "In the field of observation, chance only favors those who are prepared." This great benefactor of the human race, though loaded with honors, remained to the last simple and affectionate as a child. Pasteur was subject to fits of apoplexy and it is curious that some of his most important discoveries were made immediately after such attacks.

Darwin, from the age of thirty, was a great sufferer. His daughter writes: "No one indeed, except my mother, knows the full amount of suffering he endured, or the full amount of his wonderful patience." Dr. Darwin, however, once said to a friend: "If I had not been so great an invalid, I should not have done nearly so much work as I have accomplished."

Dr. Trudeau, who worked such miracles for the cure of consumption, was himself consumptive.

XIV
INVENTORS

Sir Richard Arkwright, the inventor of the spinning jenny, though a man of great personal strength, suffered from wretched health.

James Watt, the inventor of the steam engine, was continually ailing until he approached old age. He had a prodigious memory and as an inventive genius he has never been surpassed.

Ill health and failing eyesight forced Joseph Niepce to retire from the army at the age of twenty-eight. It was during this opportune leisure that the idea of obtaining sun-pictures first suggested itself to him. In 1826 he learnt that Daguerre was working on the same lines and three years later they cooperated in order to perfect what was, however, Niepce's discovery.

XV
HISTORIANS AND MEN OF LETTERS

Aristides, surnamed Theodosius, was a Greek rhetorician and sophist. He was so celebrated that in many places statues were erected during his lifetime to commemorate his talents. He suffered for many years from a mysterious disease, which was, however, a positive benefit to his studies as they were prescribed as part of his cure.

Pliny, the Younger, was far from robust. He suffered from weakness of the eyes, throat and chest. He himself speaks of his delicate frame.

It has been said of Erasmus that he was the first man of letters since the fall of the Roman Empire. He occupied during his lifetime the position of supreme pontiff to an elect public which the ardors of the Renaissance had called into being. His admirers were to be found in every country and among all ranks. Presents were continually sent to him by great and small. We hear of a donation of two hundred florins from Pope Clement XII and of a contribution of comfits and sweetmeats from the nuns of Cologne. From England in particular, he obtained constant supplies of money. "I receive daily," he writes, "letters from the most remote parts, from kings and princes, prelates and men of learning, and even from persons of whose existence I have never heard."

His position as regards the Reformation has been for centuries a subject of passionate contention. It was said of him, "Erasmus laid an egg, and Luther hatched it." This, however, is only partly true. As a matter of fact, Erasmus had but one passion, the passion for learning. When he found that Luther's revolt aroused a new fanaticism—that of evangelism, he recoiled from the violence of the new preachers. "Is it for this," he exclaimed, "that we have shaken off bishops and popes that we may come under the yoke of such madmen as Otto and Farel?"

Erasmus' works are too numerous to enumerate separately. His greatest contribution is undoubtedly his Greek Testament.

Erasmus spent the greater part of his life in agony. For twenty years he was unable to sit down either to read, write or even to take his meals. He could eat but little and only of the most delicate meats. He could neither eat nor bear the smell of fish. "My heart," he said, "is Catholic, but my stomach is Lutheran." Nevertheless, his various biographers exclaim at the amount of work he accomplished. One of them writes, "Through the winter of 1514–

1515 Erasmus worked with the strength of ten. In Venice ... he did the work of two men."

Montaigne was never strong but, after a few years at the court of Paris, his health gave way completely and he retired to his castle, resolved to devote the rest of his life to study and contemplation. We undoubtedly owe his immortal essays to his invalidism.

The same is true of Brantôme. He was a soldier until a fall from his horse compelled him to retire into private life. This fortunate accident is directly responsible for his "Memoirs," which are not only delightful reading but of the greatest historical value.

Fénelon, the famous tutor to the duke of Burgundy, had an enormous influence, not only on his own but on the succeeding generations. His "Treatise on the Education of Girls" guided French opinion on the subject for almost two centuries. This book brought him literary glory together with the position of tutor to the grandson and heir of Louis XIV. During the eight years at court he published the "Fables," the "Dialogues of the Dead" and finally "Télemaque." These books were intended primarily for the instruction of his pupils; they became, however, universally popular. Fénelon was banished from Paris as a result of a doctrinal difference with Bossuet. Pope Innocent XIII, while upholding the latter, gave this verdict: "Fénelon errs by loving God too much and Bossuet by loving his neighbor too little." Excessively delicate from childhood, Fénelon's health grew more and more feeble. While Archbishop of Cambrai, to which city he had retired after his disgrace, we read that he was forced to make his bed his retreat from whence to say his offices and administer his diocese.

Jean Jacques Rousseau, French "philosopher," occupied during three years of his youth the position of footman in various houses. From his own account, he made an uncommonly bad one, impertinent, mean, untruthful and dishonest! Rousseau had a most despicable character, and although he never lacked patrons, quarrelled with each in turn. Rousseau leapt into fame in 1749, when he was thirty-seven years old, by reason of an article extolling the savage over the civilized state. His two most celebrated books are "Le Contrat Social" and "La nouvelle Heloise." Only the indulgence of his contemporaries would have granted him the title of "philosopher," but as a "man of letters" he occupies "a place unrivalled in literary history." His fame, great as it was during his lifetime, reached to vertiginous heights after his death. Rousseau's health was execrable and like Voltaire it was said of him that he "was born dying."

It might have been better for Lord Chesterfield if he had not dabbled with medicine; he would perhaps not have "been so often his own patient, or entrusted his health to the care of empirics." Even before reaching middle age, his debilitated constitution had given him repeated warning of what he had to expect. When he wrote the renowned letters to his son, he was a deaf, solitary, sick man, who had to resort almost habitually to drugs to help him to endure his sufferings.

Boswell's "Life of Samuel Johnson" is so universally familiar that I need only remind you that Dr. Johnson was scrofulous and half-blind.

Horace Walpole occupied a curiously large place in the literary as well as the social life of the eighteenth century. Despite his prolific pen the only one of his books which achieved popular success during his lifetime was "The Castle of Otranto." It was translated into both French and Italian and has been frequently republished. It is a strange book, and I doubt if it will ever again be read with pleasure. Whatever significance it has for us lies in the fact that it forms the starting point of the great romantic revival. Walpole's diary, published after his death, is of the utmost historical importance. It is, however, chiefly by his letters that he will be remembered, for he is undoubtedly the greatest of the English letter-writers. Walpole suffered all his life from frequent attacks of gout which at times completely crippled him.

Winckelmann, the famous German archæologist, was the son of a poor shoemaker. He became librarian to Cardinal Passioni in 1754, and while occupying this position he gave to the world a succession of admirable books. It was from him that scholars first obtained accurate information as to the treasures excavated at Pompeii. His greatest contribution to European literature is the "History of Ancient Art." It is a delightful book, written with a free and impassioned pen and marked an epoch by "indicating the spirit in which the study of Greek art should be approached and the methods by which investigators might hope to obtain solid results." He was a great friend of Goethe and many, if not all, of their letters have been preserved. Winckelmann was so delicate that he could never partake of anything but a little bread and wine. His gentle, blameless life was cut short by the hand of a murderer, who killed him for the sake of a few ancient coins, the gift of the Empress Maria Theresa.

Herder, one of the most influential writers Germany has produced, was exceedingly delicate; so also was our own Washington Irving, which perhaps accounts for the extreme sensitiveness of the latter's impressions.

Thierry, the eminent French historian, ransacked the archives with such unremitting zeal that on the eve of beginning to write his history, he became totally blind. "But he never lost heart and in making friends with darkness," as he puts it, he returned to his work, and by means of dictation was able to finish the masterpiece that was to prove the foundation of a new school of history!... Thierry said: "If, as I believe, the progress of science is to be numbered among the glories of our land, I should again take the road that brought me to this pass. Blind and suffering, without any respite or hope of recovery, I can still witness to one point, that, coming from me, admits of no doubt; that there is something in the world of higher value than material enjoyment, nay, even than bodily health, and that is—devotion to science." Thus was the road discovered which was to be followed by Prescott, Sismondi, Macaulay and many others, including Professor Ranke.

Charles Lamb had a mental breakdown at the age of nineteen, and Mary Lamb suffered from frequent attacks of insanity.

Sir W. F. P. Napier's health was permanently injured during a campaign which carried hostilities into Spain. This obliged him to retire from the army at the age of thirty-four. This unwelcome leisure was an inestimable benefit not only to himself but to the world, as it permitted him to become the greatest military historian that England has ever produced.

Carlyle became a chronic invalid in his twenty-fourth year. The precise nature of his ailment it is impossible to ascertain, but he declared that a rat was continually gnawing at the pit of his stomach.

A most remarkable example of achievement in the face of terrible physical disabilities is presented by the historian, Francis Parkman. He was unable to open his eyes except in the dark, so that all his information had to be read aloud to him while he made notes with his eyes shut, by means of a machine he had invented as a guide to his hand. For years he suffered so intensely that half an hour's application exhausted him. The superb works he left behind, composed despite such incredible physical obstacles, have been a splendid legacy to his country.

Prescott, the eminent American historian, suffered, while at Harvard, an accident which changed the course of his life. A hard piece of bread, thrown at random in the commons hall, struck his left eye and destroyed the sight. Nevertheless he graduated honourably, but when he entered his father's office as a student of law the uninjured eye showed dangerous symptoms of inflammation. He was urged, therefore, to travel and it was at the Azores where he had to spend much of his time in a darkened room, that he "began the mental discipline which enabled him to compose and retain in memory long passages for subsequent dictation." His secretary gives this picture of him, while writing the "History of the Reign of Ferdinand and Isabella"—"seated in a study lined on two sides with books and darkened by screens of blue muslin, which required readjustment with every cloud that passed across the sky." Prescott trained his memory until he was able to retain sixty pages of printed matter, "turning and returning them as he walked or drove." After fifty his remaining eye showed serious symptoms of enfeeblement and his general health also gave cause for alarm. Nevertheless he gallantly set to work on his "History of Philip II." The third volume was, however, not through the press, before an attack of apoplexy put an end to his life.

Alfred Ainger, English divine and man of letters, chiefly remembered for his sympathetic writings on Charles Lamb and Thomas Hood, was often speechless with prostration from headaches and sickness. Ainger was no more than a charming writer. I only insert him because his handicap is one of the most difficult to overcome.

Synge, the remarkable Irish dramatist, was delicate and died young.

XVI
PROTESTANT REFORMERS

Luther stands out as the most powerful figure of the Reformation. Protestant churches of every denomination owe to him their inception, not so much on points of dogma, as because the success of his revolt made theirs possible. Luther was afflicted with epilepsy and at times from other disabilities, the exact nature of which I have been unable to ascertain. Like so many other renowned invalids, we are struck with the amount of work he accomplished. During the last ten years of his life he suffered from continuous ill health, yet he spent them in incessant labor. He was preaching with vehemence and fervor on February 19, 1546, when suddenly he said, quietly, "This and much more is to be said about the Gospel; but I am too weak and will close here." Four days later he was dead.

Calvin suffered constant bodily pain, yet he was a man of incessant activity and of supreme courage. At one time, not only the council but the people of Geneva revolted against his authority; a riot was imminent. Calvin at once set out alone for the council-chamber where he was greeted with yells and threats of death. Advancing slowly into their midst he bared his breast, saying: "If you will have blood, strike here!" Not an arm moved and, turning his back on his enemies, he slowly mounted the stairs to the tribune.

John Knox began his career as a Catholic priest and we have so little knowledge of his early life that we are ignorant as to what occasioned the startling change in his views. After his accession to the ranks of Protestantism he had at first no idea of preaching but confined himself to instructing his friends' children. His friends, however, recognized his capacity and on his refusing "to run where God had not called him," they planned a solemn appeal to Knox from the pulpit to accept "the public office and charge of preaching." At the close of this exhortation Knox burst into tears and shut himself in his chamber, "in heaviness, for many days." The call had at last found a leader of men. Yet it was an invitation to danger and to death. Shortly afterwards St. Andrews was attacked by the French fleet and Knox was among the prisoners taken. He was thrown into a galley and for nineteen months remained in irons and subject to the lash. When he was finally released, he was a man almost forty-five years old and completely broken in health, by reason of the hardships and cruelty to which he had been subjected. Yet his career was only just beginning. "To Knox more than to any other man Scotland owes her religion and individuality." He was of great political importance and one of the most powerful enemies of Maria Stuart. As an historian he occupies an important place. His "History of the Reformation in Scotland" is a remarkable book. It was said of him "he neither flattered nor feared any flesh." He was an inspired preacher. Elizabeth's very critical ambassador wrote from Edinburgh that "this one man was able in one hour to put more life in us than five hundred trumpets."

Richard Baxter was diseased from head to foot; nevertheless, he became celebrated as the most eminent of the English Protestant schoolmen. He was also of political importance and instrumental in bringing about the Restoration of Charles II.

XVII
THE SAINTS

"When we look into God's Face we do not feel His Hand."

Health is a form of capital, and like any other capital may be either well or ill invested. Moreover, we can squander it foolishly or convert it into the supreme oblation, and to most of us life itself is a less difficult sacrifice. The tragedy of war is not so much the toll of the dead as the lists of the disabled.

Few of us are given the chance of dying for others, but to all of us is offered the privilege of spending ourselves for humanity, either individually or collectively. Countless parents, fathers as well as mothers, purchase with their own lives and health, life, vigor and opportunity for their children. The instinct of sacrifice is to a greater or less degree universal to parenthood, and although I do not wish to belittle their offering, I think it even more admirable when placed on a less obvious altar. Numberless people are daily overspending their physical resources in the service of mankind, by the furtherance of knowledge, the improvement of material conditions, by widening the door of opportunity or carrying the message of the spirit into teeming slum and arid desert. Others give themselves with equal prodigality in the more limited and less glorious field of their personal contacts; not merely to their homes, their dependents and friends but to all who come even casually within the radius of their fellowship.

It seems to me difficult to live at the height of our possibilities more especially if our activities are purely selfless, without being at times tempted to overdraw our health account. The soldier is only one of a great host whose bodies have been sacrificed in the performance of an imperative duty. Health is often purchased at the price of ignominious refusal.

It is therefore not surprising that a large proportion of the saints were men and women with ruined bodies,—bodies that had been rapturously spent in the service of God and man. I will mention only a few of the most renowned.

St. Jerome, one of the greatest of the early Christian Fathers, lived an unregenerate life until a severe illness induced a complete change in him and he resolved to renounce everything that kept him back from God. His greatest temptation was the study of the literature of Greece and pagan Rome, and he determined from thenceforth to devote all his vast scholarship to the Holy Scriptures and to Christianity. To him we owe the first translation of the Bible into Latin, commonly known as the "Vulgate."

Very few men have ever wielded greater power over the minds of men than St. Augustine. He is to-day a living force, yet he struggled all his life against consumption. He lived, however, to be seventy-six.

St. Bernard of Clairvaux, the most famous monk and preacher of the Middle Ages, was a martyr to so many physical infirmities that at first sight he appeared "like one near unto death." All this suffering, however, never quelled his ardent spirit or his overmastering zeal for purging the world of sin. It was St. Bernard who said, "Nothing can work me damage but myself; the harm I sustain I carry about with me, and I am never a real sufferer but by my own fault."

St. Francis of Assisi was a gay, dissipated youth when a severe illness put a stop to his pleasures, and gave him time to reflect, so that he became dissatisfied with his mode of life. On his recovery he set out on a military expedition, but at the end of the first day's march he fell ill and had to return to Assisi. This disappointment brought on another spiritual crisis and shortly afterwards he went on a pilgrimage to Rome. Before everything he was an ascetic and a mystic,—an ascetic who though gentle to others wore out his body in self-denial, so much so that when he came to die, he begged pardon of "brother Ass, the body," for having unduly ill-treated it.

St. Catherine of Siena was not only a very great saint, but one of the greatest women that ever lived. The daughter of a poor dyer who learned to read when she was twenty and to write when she was twenty-seven or eight, she dictated books and letters celebrated not only for their spiritual fragrance and literary value, but also for their great historical importance. No empress ever wielded greater power than this extraordinary woman. Towards the end of her life her court consisted of pilgrims who flocked daily by the thousands to visit her. The miracle of her personality had its effect on all who approached her. A young libertine, belonging to one of the most aristocratic families of Siena, after one interview with this dyer's daughter, abandoned his former life and became her humble follower until the day of her death. She converted a notorious robber, who for years terrorized the vicinity of Siena and had almost paralyzed its commerce. As a proof of the sincerity of his repentance he gave her his stronghold, together with all the spoils he had accumulated. The abandonment of Avignon as the seat of the Papal court undoubtedly changed not only the map, but also the history of Europe, and it was solely owing to St. Catherine's passionate insistence that Pope Gregory XI returned to Rome, despite his own reluctance and the opposition of his cardinals. During her short life she was continually ill and during the period of her greatest activity she was dying.

St. Ignatius Loyola, one of the most remarkable and influential personages in the history of the Catholic Church, led the adventurous life of a courtier and a soldier until he received a wound at the siege of Pamplona. According to an old chronicler this "was the occasion of his conversion to God." A cannon-ball hit his legs, shattering one. Serious illness followed the most painful operation, and for weeks his life was despaired of. It was on the bed of torment which he eventually left, lame for life and constitutionally enfeebled, that grace came to him. The saint himself said, when he returned from the Valley of the Shadow: "I have seen God face to face and my soul has been saved." From that time onward he devoted himself to a spiritual life, wandering far and accomplishing much. Chief among his achievements was the founding of the Order of Jesuits. I must mention here a very remarkable fact that has, however, nothing to do with my thesis. In his will he bequeathed to the order he founded this legacy: "that all men should speak ill of it." It is also curious that he who had benefited by illness should have said: "A sound mind in a sound body is the most useful instrument with which to serve God."

St. Theresa of Jesus, the great Spanish saint, whose personality and writings have never lost their influence, was always extremely delicate, and during the period of her greatest accomplishments not only ill but old.

With St. Theresa closes my list of those gallant souls who, apparently unfit for the battle of life, have nevertheless left their mark on history and civilization. And I wish to remind you again that I have mentioned no one whose height of achievement has not been coincident with ill-health, or reached after the suffering of some serious physical disability. Neither have I thought it proper to cite any of the numerous instances of handicapped genius among our living contemporaries.

I am certain that many other names might be presented to your consideration, if it were not for my own ignorance as well as the extreme difficulty of getting any reliable data on the subject.

XVIII
PAIN, THE GREAT TEACHER

"What does he know," said a sage, "who has not suffered?"

That we may be benefited by physical suffering is no new idea,—it is not even a forgotten idea. From the time when civilization first expressed itself in terms of Christianity until the Reformation, the spiritual value of pain has been an undisputed axiom. The Catholic Church has never ceased to preach the mortification of the flesh, and all religious communities, heathen as well as Christian, consider a certain degree of asceticism necessary for the perfect manifestation of a spiritual life.

As to the merits of voluntary suffering inflicted for the purpose of subjugating the appetites of the body, Christendom differs fundamentally, but until recently, it has been united in regarding illness as one of the means by which Providence purifies as well as punishes its children.

The discovery of the germ, even more than the preaching of Mrs. Eddy, dealt a terrific blow to this ancient belief, with the result that the masses no longer regard physical suffering as a remedial agency but as something not only unprofitable but purely destructive. For more than thirty years the final abolition of pain has been the Mecca towards which doctors and Christian Scientists have passionately journeyed; moreover, their ranks have been swelled by numerous sects, schools or religious bodies that have been called into existence by the rallying cry of this New Hope. They pointed to the declining death rate as an irrefutable testimony of battles already won, and as disease after disease disappeared before the advance of sanitation, of serums or of Right Thought; as surgery developed unheard-of possibilities, the most limitless expectations seemed not unjustified. The natural infirmities of age must eventually yield before the onslaught of knowledge. Bolder spirits even dreamed of conquest over death.

And then the World War came.

Their boasted death-rate mounted to unheard-of heights. The maimed and blind overflowed from the hospitals unto the farthest corners of the earth. Still the havoc was not complete. Infantile paralysis came from the north, killing and crippling our children by thousands. Finally, influenza mowed down old and young in such numbers that even here in America it was impossible to care for all the victims.

One would have expected these facts to be a staggering blow to our theorists. Could they not have realized—if only dimly—that they were battling against some fundamental law? Evidently not, for according to them war is to be abolished. Not only that, but Dr. Voronoff now offers an infallible cure for old age!

Now, as I said before, I neither believe that physical suffering will ever be abolished nor do I even hope it. For pain is one of the great human and humanizing experiences and, since the beginning of time, each generation has learned in its school the same fundamental lessons.

"When a man is laboring under the pain of any distemper it is then that he recollects there is a God and that he is but a man. No mortal is then the object of his envy, his admiration or his contempt; and, having no malice to gratify, the tales of slander excite him not." This is the testimony of a heathen, Pliny, who was himself an invalid. Sixteen centuries later an Anglican divine, Jeremy Taylor, voiced a similar conviction. "In sickness the soul begins to dress herself for immortality. At first she unties the strings of vanity that made her upper garments cleave to the world and sit uneasy."

Even during the materialistic nineteenth century we find Dr. Samuel Smiles declaring: "Suffering is doubtless as divinely appointed as joy, while it is much more influential as a discipline of character. It chastens and sweetens the nature, teaches patience and resignation and promotes the deepest as well as the most exalted thoughts."

Latterly there have been indications that this time-honored conception is again becoming more universally recognized. For instance, during the darkest days of the war the Bishop of London writes that he had "come to believe that a painless world is a world not regenerate but degenerate."

Who shall say that the revival of religious feeling which is now taking place is not due to the physical and mental suffering entailed by the war?

I should like to linger on the spiritual value of suffering, yet I feel I am on very delicate ground. For the spirit is so gloriously independent of the flesh, that it can expand under any circumstances and in any habitation. St. Hildegarde believed "God could not dwell in a healthy body," and St. Ignatius Loyola that "a healthy mind in a healthy body is the best instrument with which to serve God." Yet he himself had a shattered body.

The efficacy of suffering in promoting the growth of the spirit seems to me to lie chiefly in the fact that it does for us what we so seldom have the courage to do for ourselves. It sweeps away all the rubbish and dust of life. In the blessed emptiness induced by this mental house-cleaning we are able, often for the first time, to separate clearly the essential from the unessential. In sickness soul and body demand instinctively only that which is for each its most imperative necessity.

In the crucible of suffering the true essence of our character becomes manifest. All our pitiable pretences are torn from us, leaving our inherent self face to face with reality. It is a tremendous experience; it must either break us or make us. It is for us to choose which it shall be. Suffering is the ultimate test of character.

Yet as I write these words I find myself wondering if there is any one ultimate test. As no two crystals react to the same solvent, so it may be that no two hearts respond to the same probe. Of one thing, nevertheless, I am certain: to each of us is applied at some time in our lives that which constitutes for that individual soul the supreme trial of its mettle.

I am frequently reminded, however, that there are countless people who, instead of being purified and sensitized by physical pain, have been destroyed or at least rendered sterile by it. This is undoubtedly true. Whether we are to profit by suffering or not depends entirely on ourselves. How then are we to transmute pain into privilege? Certainly not through resignation, for there is no virtue without action. It may only be the interior travail of the spirit, but to attain even the initial step to spiritual, intellectual or material advancement necessitates labor. So it is with the benefits of suffering. They are there within the reach of all, but can only be obtained as the wage of persistent endeavor.

Resignation is not merely inactive, it is positively harmful inasmuch as it is a tacit acknowledgment that pain is in itself an evil, and to believe that is to stultify its possibilities. For what we believe to be evil, no matter how innocent in itself, becomes so by the corrosive power of that belief.

It is a dogma of Christianity that disease is one of the punitive consequences of original sin. Now punishment implies correction. Therefore, if disease represents a fall from perfection, it also holds within it the germs of a future perfection. Although theology teaches sin as the inception of disease, yet if we consider only the immediate cause of our physical disabilities we will find that although they are frequently the result of breaking a moral law, they are quite as frequently to be attributed to no fault of our own, and may even be the emblem of sacrifice.

If so many fail to benefit through suffering, we must remember that only a few of us are able to sustain the daily test of life. Every experience, especially any great and unusual experience, is a fire through which few pass unscathed. Beauty, charm, riches, personality, even intellect, have each their separate temptation, their different limitations.

It is so easy for the spirit to sleep contented within the soft prison of a perfect body. Superabundant health and vitality, unless guided by infinite wisdom, are as likely to cast us into the abyss of life as to raise us to the summit. Power fosters pride, and charm is the twin-sister of vanity. Life is a continuous trial of our strength, but disease is not necessarily the supreme trial.

It was George Eliot who said: "There is nothing the body suffers the soul may not profit by."

XIX
CONCLUSION

Who best can suffer, best can do.

—*Milton.*

We have seen that as mankind rises in the scale of civilization the body becomes increasingly less important. Nevertheless, I wish it to be clearly understood, that I do not maintain that it is preferable to be ill than well, but only that each state has its own peculiar privileges, which are rarely interchangeable.

Health and sickness are merely different roads to achievement. The earth requires rain as well as sunshine; we need both tears and laughter; navvies are necessary and so are philosophers.

You may therefore reasonably ask why, if suffering is indispensable to humanity, doctors and sociologists should spend themselves and their lives in attempting to banish it from the world?

Because, if pain is the gate through which we must pass to attain certain experiences and realizations, to battle against it is undoubtedly the road to others. To endure pain and to relieve pain are both instrumental in freeing us from the prison of ourselves, and freedom from self is the only real freedom. Moreover, whatever ameliorates human conditions, whether serums or sanitation, free concerts or fireless cookers, results in loosing us from the thraldom of the body.

The race reaches toward an ideal of ultimate perfection, just as a plant stretches upward towards the sun. Both are unattainable, yet all activity would cease, if we demanded nothing less than absolute and indestructible achievement. The tide flows only to ebb, the field must be sown anew year after year; we build cities knowing that time will eventually destroy them; we bear children doomed to death.

But after the ebb comes the tide, bringing ever new treasures to our shores; the germ of spring lies hidden in the barren breast of autumn; out of the ashes of vast cities still greater cities will arise, and Death is but the portal of Life.

No physical disablement is a barrier to achievement. This is the glorious fact which the illustrious men and women I have enumerated have proved beyond the possibility of dispute. To cripple and hunchback, to blind, deaf and dumb, to those chained to "a mattress-grave," and to those who have been mentally unbalanced, they have bequeathed this precious legacy of Hope.

On the other hand we can no longer plead our infirmities as an excuse for our weakness, our sterility or failure. For whatever may be our disablement we can find in history a parallel debility triumphantly transmuted into strength.

THE END

Milton Keynes UK
Ingram Content Group UK Ltd.
UKHW030627061024
449204UK00004B/260